Life

Love

Laughter

by

Del Pope

Published by Levin Publishing Group LLC

Copyright © 2007 by Del Pope   All rights reserved

No part of this publication may be reproduced, stored in a retrieval system, or transmitted in any form or by any means, electronic, mechanical, photocopying, recording, scanning, or otherwise without written permission from the author.

Edition: 10 9 8 7 6 5 4 3 2 1   SAN: 256-8799

Library of Congress Control Number: 2007939106

ISBN-10: 0-9771431-6-3
ISBN-13: 978-0-9771431-6-0

Printed and Bound in United States of America

Cover design by Lillian Semanski

DEDICATION

This book is dedicated to my family
and all of my friends, past, present and future.

I also want thank my daughter Dee Ann Pope
for helping me with my computer and for her poems
which are included in this book.

And To Lillian Semanski for her support
and her poem.

A very special thank you to Nancy King for her
constant encouragement and direction.

AUTHOR'S NOTE

My poetry is written for content and pleasure
rather than form and style.

Life - Love - Laughter
Del Pope

HAPPINESS

Happiness is an attitude
Attitudes can be assumed
Why not assume the attitude of happiness
And be happy

Life - Love - Laughter
Del Pope

ONE DAY AT A TIME

You live one day at a time my dear
Yesterday is gone forever and
Tomorrow is not yet here.

One day at a time, you need have no
fear - For yesterday is to be
forgotten and Tomorrow is not yet
in gear.

One day at a time, today is for real.
Enjoy it to it's fullest -
Let your old wounds heal.

One day at a time
'Tis enough for you to carry

ONE DAY AT A TIME.

Life - Love - Laughter
Del Pope

TO LOVE A FRIEND

To love a friend is kind of special
Regardless of the gender

It happens to us now and then
As relationships we enter.

So why not foster these good moments
And give ourselves to others.

Why not treat our fellowman
As though they all are brothers

Life - Love - Laughter
Del Pope

LIVE EACH DAY

Live each day to its' fullest
And never let it die
Until you have gleaned all that you can
And give it your best try.
It's easy to say what's the use
While sitting in the shade
But the world is moved and destinies shaped
By the efforts man has made.

Life - Love - Laughter
Del Pope

INTROSPECT

This poem is writ in introspect,
As it has been requested
Although I'm not so sure
Enough of life's digested --
To help me look inside of me
And I'm not sure I'll like
The picture I will see.

I think *that* brings us all some dread.
We think we'd rather, first, be dead.
Well, anyway, my mind is clear Why I
came to Laguna.
I had to start a whole new life,
I felt like a beginner.
New friends I've found
And also a new talent
Without financial woes
I'd be real content.

I like to write the poems I hear
Through my poetic antenna
I'd rather write a real good poem
Than eat a well cooked dinner.
So, suffer me, if you will,

Another line or two,
While I try to make more clear The
one addressing you
It's not so easy, it's just like work To
sit upon this stool --
And try to write in introspect
And not reveal a fool.

Life - Love - Laughter
Del Pope

Aren't we all a little weak --
And don't we try to hide it Well, like
they   say, let it all hang out,
You don't know, if you haven't tried it. I
have a feeling this won't work,
My antenna is a failin'
Because myself is freezing up,
My defenses are prevailin'

Life - Love - Laughter
Del Pope

TO LISA A CHLORASEPTIC JUNKIE

I'm a Chloraseptic junkie
But, it's all that I can do.
I cough and hack and pop a
lozenge To fight this crazy flu
The doctor said about three weeks
I don't know if I can stand it.
Maybe if I smile a lot
I'll make out like a bandit.
My stomach hurts and I may have
A great big ulcer, peptic
But I've just got to keep on
working So, I pop a Chloraseptic.

Life - Love - Laughter
Del Pope

IRS/GESTAPO

Who can take all you own
And do it with much gall.

Who can take a whole paycheck
And leave no food at all.

Who can cause a heart attack
And not a doctor call

Who can cause a breakdown
And watch you while you fall.

There are two such groups
That you and I know.

Internal Revenue Service
And the German Gestapo

Life - Love - Laughter
Del Pope

DEAR MOM and DAD

Where have the years gone
Since I was young
And you were teaching
Me how not to get stung
Both by bees
And life's ugly barbs
Or playing uninvited
In other people's yards
How swift the years Have
gone forever
It's too late now
Just to be clever
For life has a way
To broaden your view
While teaching you how
To find the real you
First we are up
And then we are down
But we learn soon
To not wear a frown
For people draw near
Whenever you smile
But drift away
If a frown is your style

Life - Love - Laughter
Del Pope

BIG BEAR LAKE

The pines are so beautiful and green and tall
Reaching toward the sky
The green and blue and the gold of the sun
Bring pleasure to my eye.

It's quiet and still and so peaceful here
As the squirrels scamper and play.
The blue jays tease them and steal their food,
It makes the blue jays day.

They are pretty. Their feathers are so blue, I
am sure you love them too.
Each morning when you wake,
You have the feeling
Of life brand new

The lake is so tranquil
With boats around it's edge,
'Til winter's snows bring people
With skis and sleds

The people seem so happy
With cheeks and noses red
It's much more fun at Big Bear
Than lying home in bed

Life - Love - Laughter
Del Pope

LOVE REQUITED

In the glow of love requited
My heart's halo you have lighted
Giving me such sweet repast
I hope it will forever last

When I look into your eyes
The best within me seems to rise
And all my hopes and all my dreams
Are so full they burst their seams

For one to have such inspiration
Is like the beginning of creation
One can soar just like an eagle
And gain such heights of feelings regal

Isn't this what makes worth while
All the risk of childlike guile
To give one's heart to another
With no reserve - to soar and hover

To trust and love and give your best
And trust it will forever last
So why not love with heart and soul
And try to reach the elusive goal

Of perfect love and perfect trust
That transcends feelings even lust.

Life - Love - Laughter
Del Pope

DORIS

This is for Doris
A very good friend
I hope she'll remain
To the very end

Our paths are similar
But not the same
Or maybe I'm
Just hard to tame

Well anyway
This much I know
No other is like her
Where ever I go

She seems to care
And seems so loyal
Even though I'm
Not rich with oil

Or any other
Worldly goods
To put her in
Some better moods

Or offer her
Some fancy fashion
To send her spirit
Upward dashin'

Well, I'm just me
So here I am
I'm glad that she
Does give a damn

Life - Love - Laughter
Del Pope

CHRISTMAS CHEER

Christmas cheer is all around
So keep your feet upon the ground
Don't spend too much money
Don't go into debt
Or this time next year
You'll be paying yet

Then it's time to spend again
You'll be in debt up to your chin
But spread good cheer
And spread your love
You'll get a blessing
From up above

Life - Love - Laughter
Del Pope

THE GOOD YEARS

I remember the good years,
Rather than the bad
The good years were the ones
The most of which we had

The laughing, the joking,
The loving we shared ---
We couldn't say enough
How much we cared.

Sorrow and pain were shared
And soon we came to know
These made love fonder
And deeper roots to grow

No, it's not too late
I now can see
To say these things,
And you'll agree ---

For life goes on
And not for aught,
But, to share the good years
That life hath wrought.

Sure there was bad
And we know well ---
To live through it
Was a living hell

But, love and beauty
Are here to stay,
In spite of all

That we may say.

Life - Love - Laughter
Del Pope

The good years remain
Forever, in memory,
To comfort and bring
Pleasure 'til eternity

When a new love With no
pain or sorrows,
Greets us with eternally
Bright tomorrows

Life - Love - Laughter
Del Pope

A DAUGHTER NAMED DEE

I have a daughter who's name is Dee.
She's very close to the heart of me.
She is so often in my thought,
Though with life's worries I am fraught

To hear her call can make me happy,
And make me feel a bit more carefree.
Oh, I know sometimes she calls
To say, "Hi Dad ", and then she bawls;

And tells me of some care or other
That has become more than a bother.
But, most of all she calls to say,
"I thought of you three times today."

And she has been a daughter, loyal,
And makes me feel so very royal
For this is one of life's great pleasures;
In your child's eyes to see the measures -

Of love and real appreciation -
And to fulfill their expectation
Of you as parent and confidante,
No matter what your child may want

So, God help me when she may call -
Give my paternal, loving all
To lighten up her dreary day;
Help me to find just what to say;

And she in turn will lighten mine
And make my sun begin to shine.

Life - Love - Laughter
Del Pope

FLU

Feeling low and kind of cranky?
Blowing your nose on your hanky?
Have you got that old flu bug?
Need to get a great big hug?
Well, I care and wish you well,
That old flu can go to hell.
I'll stand by and help you blow ---
DID YOU SAY FLU? I gotta go!

I'M A LEAF

Hi. Look up here
I'm a leaf on a tree

I'm green and fresh
And happy as can be

I wave in the wind
And give my friends shade

I'm glad God decided
That I should be made

Life - Love - Laughter
Del Pope

ODE TO MARY NEWLANDS

Your kindness is a breath of air So
fresh and sweet and clean Though I
have traveled far and wide It's the
freshest I have seen

So gentle and considerate
So thoughtful and so kind
I think I shall look no more
One kinder I'll not find

Life - Love - Laughter
Del Pope

POETRY

Poetry is such a pleasure
A way to communicate
Whether comical or serious
Your statement you can make

Some poems are hilarious
Some are so serene
Some are about reality
Some are about a dream

What a privilege to be able
To express ones self that way
It sometimes makes the
difference Between a good or
ho-hum day

Life - Love - Laughter
Del Pope

RAINBOW

The most beautiful sight
That I have seen
Is the colors of a rainbow
When the world is clean

The rain has come
And washed our world
The green foliage
Is now unfurled

The flowers erect
Raise their heads
Their beauty is radiant
In their moist beds

My eyes are happy
My nose is pleased
My problems are dimmer
My minds at ease

Life - Love - Laughter
Del Pope

SEARCH FOR TRUE LOVE

Search for true love
It's worth the trip
A true love companion
Will give your life zip

With zest and gusto
Your days will be great
If you have found
Your real life's mate

Life - Love - Laughter
Del Pope

THE SEA AND ME

The sea will roll
Forever more
From where I am
To a distant shore
Its' waves will forever
Restless be
For there's always motion
In the sea

The tides will come
And then they'll ebb
'Sorta' like a spider
Spinning a web
But the spider soon
Will finish his
While the sea goes on
With a roar and a hiss

As breakers come
And crash to shore
I think of many
Days of yore
With pirates and ships
And men and goods
In ships of steel
And ships of wood

With guns ablazin'
And swords aflashin'
Here and there a lady In
the latest fashion

Life - Love - Laughter
Del Pope

Maybe some day
I'll roam some more
Where rolling waves break
On a mysterious shore,

To have an adventure
Of my very own
And need never more
To leave my home

Life - Love - Laughter
Del Pope

ODE TO HELEN

This ode's to Helen
A real nice lady
Who shares my time
When she is ready

Her charm is different
And rather lean
I think one night
She was in my dream

When I awoke
I said to me
Was it really Helen
That I could see

Well I'm not sure
But this I know
If she's there again
I'm ready to go

Life - Love - Laughter
Del Pope

MY DEAR OLD DAD

My dear old dad is something else
But I will tell you this

To see his smile and twinkling eye
Is 'sorta' like a kiss

With all respect I this can say
His kiss is rarer than bonny day

He's so reserved and kind of shy
But he'll look a man right in the eye

To know him is to love him many will agree
Even his in-laws long his face to see

And when one calls whom he loves
And says I need some help

His calm will hold and you won't hear
A whine or a yelp

His deeds are all done
Without a horn a blarin'

Cause no one needs to know
What it is he's sharin'

If he loves you count it lucky
For his loves are few

That he will talk about, that is
Lucky if one is you

Life - Love - Laughter
Del Pope

For then you are a privileged person
At least in my opinion

For he's the finest Dad
In Gods great big dominion

LOW EBB

In the quiet of my room,
Sinking deeper in my gloom,
My very soul seems to ache,
While self analysis I make.

Is it true that I'd feel better
If I had followed to the letter,
All the things my parents taught,
Or, would I still be distraught?

Am I the cause of this feeling?
Is someone else my comfort stealing?
Is it wise to search so inward
Or, should I start to climb upward?

My mind seems a total mess
But, I have learned, more or less,
That time will help to improve
My lot in life and brow to soothe

Life - Love - Laughter
Del Pope

JANE JANE

Jane Jane What a pain
I hate to write
This thing inane
But do it now I really must
For I must not betray the trust
Of my antenna which does rise
With inspiration toward the skies
For when it rises I must write
Whether midday or midnight

So now that I am in this dither
The question now is when or whether
I should tell the truth I see
She really was a pain to me
Though I would make progress
She would say "Now let's digress-
For now I think it should be thus."
And with a lot of needless fuss
She would make a lot of major changes
And put my emotions into distress

Why should I plan and help
If every day she would yelp

I changed my mind so let's do this.
Let that go for now I miss
A way to go in from the rainy wet
We haven't solved that problem yet.

"Let's build a stair or yet a bed.
Before it's done I'll be dead
For I can't stand the derision
Of my mind with her decision"
Because tomorrow it will change
And I will bet it even rains

Life - Love - Laughter
Del Pope

HELLO

Well hello I'm glad to see you
It's been quite a while
Since I've seen your face
And winning sunny smile

I've really missed your presence
And needed to renew
The many pleasant hours
I enjoyed so with you
And who do I mean
Whenever I say you
I mean the other me
Who was absent and so blue

Life - Love - Laughter
Del Pope

BECKEY- THE COBBLER AND THE ELF

A lady named Beckey

Was sitting one day

In Spectrum Spas

And I happened to say,

"You've a run in your stocking."

And to my surprise

No tears came welling

Into her eyes,

For instead there was tolerance

And a great big smile

And much control all the while.

I think she was saying

To her fine self,

"Forgive this cobbler,
Or, is he an elf?"

Life - Love - Laughter
Del Pope

DARE TO DREAM

Dare to dream. Dare to try.
Dare to challenge to do or die.
Dare to think that it's possible
That your ideas may be plausible
To succeed or fail is up to you
Give it a whirl and when you're through,
You'll find more darings and then you'll do
The things you always wanted to.
Nothing ventured, nothing gained,
Give it a go, be not detained.
Dare to dream, dare to try,
Raise your sights to the sky.
DREAM and DO!!

Life - Love - Laughter
Del Pope

WILL I LOVE AGAIN

Will I dare to love again

Will I risk the hurt

Will I dare to trust again

And marry in a church

Can my heart and mind survive

The feelings o so deep

If someone fails again

Their promises to keep

Life - Love - Laughter
Del Pope

THE WAY SHE LOOKS TO ME

I've met a lot of women
Since becoming a single guy

But this one seems mysterious
Quiet reserved and shy

I can't tell what she is thinking
And I don't know how to act

I want her to know me
And that's an actual fact

But how can I present myself
With my best foot forward

When by her quiet demeanor
She makes me feel so awkward

I think of the nicest things
I want to say to her

Then I stammer and stutter
And it all comes out absurd

Is it that I want her so
Or that I am perplexed

Does she think that I'm a fool
Or maybe oversexed

I've got to break the ice
I'm sure I'll find a way

Life - Love - Laughter
Del Pope

To keep from sounding foolish
And maybe save the day

Well I'll just keep on trying
If it's to be it will click

If not I'll come off looking
Like another country hick

Life - Love - Laughter
Del Pope

SAN DIEGO AT NIGHT

San Diego at night
And no place to go
I long for the sight
Of someone I know
Sitting in Littlefield's
Watching the buses
And a sign that says yield
Some people make fusses
While waiting their turn
To get on their coach
A girl starts to burn
At one guy's approach
I guess it's time
To go to the inn
And get some sleep
Let tomorrow begin

Life - Love - Laughter
Del Pope

TRIBUTE TO MARY NEWLANDS

Mary Dear, wherever you are,
Whether here or a distant star,

Know I love you and miss you so,
Wherever in the universe you may go

You always made my way much brighter
And the cloudiest day seem much lighter.

To hear your voice when you'd call
Would pick me up from any fall.

Your smile and your gentle tone
Were true in person or on the phone

I've only known you for about a year.
So quickly you've become extra dear.

Your concern had such consistence,
Whether close, or at a distance.

And to be with you at the wedding in the park
Was a ray of bright sunlight shining in the dark

Your gentleness and sincerity
Were often in my reverie

While your music was so special,
Your love in it was ethereal.

I see you now in lush green valleys,
With sunshine and no back alleys,

Life - Love - Laughter
Del Pope

Where everything is so much better
I wish you could write me a letter.

Or better yet to telephone
And hear your voice while I'm alone.

Nothing else can take its place.
Your friendship was like the finest lace,

Given with love and consideration
For one to treasure in meditation.

My love goes out in a truly rare way,
For the day I met Mary was a finer day.

Life - Love - Laughter
Del Pope

HAPPY MOTHER'S DAY M K

Happy Mother's Day Mary K

Your children have been blessed

With a mother who sacrificed

And cared

Through the severest test

To raise your children by yourself

And do it well you did

Was quite an undertaking

And now it can be said

You are a mother worthy of

Your children's deepest love

May this Mother's Day bring blessings

From your Father up above

Life - Love - Laughter
Del Pope

EXCEPTIONAL PERSON

You are one exceptional person I've met

Who hears the bells ringing yet

Way after Christmas through each day

You smile a greeting and you say

Peace and love in your soul

To last forever while eternities roll

Life - Love - Laughter
Del Pope

A MISTAKE OF LOVE

I told her that I loved her,
As I had since we were wed,
That if early I should cease to be
I'd be happier wherever I was
If only I could see
She was with someone like Bill.

He would be loving kind and true
And treat my Honey like I always tried
and wanted to.
And, I added with a smile,
That I had better first be dead

Then time passed and one day,
Much to my surprise,
My Darling told me
She would separate our lives.
She wanted to live alone, she said,
And out of my control,
And soon she was gone
And I was feeling old.

I'd never known such dark despair
And utter loneliness,
Without my Darlings arms around me
In tender sweet caress.
Ere long I discovered to my surprise
(Or had I been misled),
She was living in Hawaii with Bill
And I wasn't even dead.

Had my deep love and concern for her
Planted a seed too soon
Telling her Bill was right for her,

Life - Love - Laughter
Del Pope

If I should die too soon
Was it too much for her to bear
Seeing him every day
And knowing I thought
Of her with him,
If God took me away

Was it a mistake of love
Wrought by my concern
I didn't want her to be alone
And feel as I do now,
Because I loved her so

Life - Love - Laughter
Del Pope

CHRISTMAS IN CALIFORNIA

Snow is not blowing
Green grass is growing
It's Christmas in California

Still, Santa is coming
Toy drums are drumming
It's Christmas in California

The lights are so bright
They're such a joyful sight
It's Christmas in California

So be of good cheer
With people who are dear
It's Christmas in California

PEACEFUL EVENING

Evening has come
The sun is setting
Dew the flowers
Now is wetting

The hedge is damp
The lawn is moist
The evening bliss
Is giving voice

Sit and relax
Be at ease
Feel the warmth
Of the evening breeze

Know that God
Is up above
Showering you
With eternal love

Life - Love - Laughter
Del Pope

JUDY G

My first born was Judy G.
'Twas Father's Day she came to me.
My very first Father's Day,
She came to brighten up my way.

And soon a new tradition came.
Birthdays would never be the same.
When she was asked what kind of cake
She wanted her mother now to bake,

Her reply came swift and sure,
"I want watermelon simple and pure."
"But where," we said, "do we put the candles
And watermelons don't have handles."

But she replied so very sweet,
" Just stick the candles in the meat
And do it quickly, 'cause I can't wait
To have birthday watermelon
Instead of birthday cake"

Life - Love - Laughter
Del Pope

BIRTHDAYS

Birthdays come and birthdays go
And some are better by far

I hope the one you're having now
Makes you younger than you are

Life - Love - Laughter
Del Pope

HERPES SIMPLEX PARANOIA
(Fever Blisters)

Herpes is a disease
That strikes terror
In some hearts
It does sound bad
According to medical reports
But it has engendered
Another affliction
About which I'll tell ya
I call it H.P. for short
It stands for Herpes Paranoia
I know it's only a cold sore
But please
Don't 'cha kiss me
No please
Don't shake my hand
You may infectious be
Yes I love you and I care
But please
Don't even touch me
Excuse me for a moment
I must go brush my teeth
From Herpes paranoia
I must find relief
I'm losing all my friends
Can hardly conduct my business
I'm so paralyzed
By their Dizziness
Is it worse to have the disease
Or is it better for ya
To suffer ten thousand deaths
With Herpes Paranoia

Life - Love - Laughter
Del Pope

I LOVE YOU

I love you

I love you

I love you

I'll shout it to the world

I'll write it on a banner

To fly on high unfurled

I want all to know I love you

And will 'til the end of time

I love you

I love you

I love you

Please say that you are mine

Life - Love - Laughter
Del Pope

I BELIEVE

I believe, there is a Supreme Being.

I believe, He/She/It set the forces of nature in place.

I believe, for the most part, we control our own destiny.

I believe, if we make diligent effort to better ourselves in any way, the forces of nature come into play to aid us.

I believe, people are mistaken when they blame God for their misfortune. Things happen by the forces of nature and/or the actions of our selves or others.

I believe, children are a natural result of copulation, not a blessing or curse from God.

I believe, God has a sense of humor. He gave us one.

I believe, God is the spirit of love.

I believe, we should love each other.

I believe, it is wrong to have more children than you can provide for and educate properly.

I believe we should help ourselves and each other.

I believe, if lightning strikes you it is a hap

stance of nature.

I believe, earthquakes are a natural phenomenon, not a sign from God. The same is true for volcanoes, floods, pestilence, and disease.

I believe, if good people strive for good they will, in the end, prevail.

Life - Love - Laughter
Del Pope

BEVERLY HARNDEN

Beverly, dear, we want you to know
We're here to cheer you on.

On balance beam and uneven bars
You can be number one.

On floor or vault, give it your best
And reach for a star.

But keep your feet upon the ground
We love you for who you are.

Life - Love - Laughter
Del Pope

HAPPY BIRTHDAY MARY D

Happy birthday Mary
You are such a delight

Many happy returns
And peaceful sleep at night

May your next year be better
The way you want it to

And rest assured that I
Will still be thinking of you

LIGHT OF MY LIFE

Guardian Angel

Light of my life

How often I've thought of you as my wife

You are there when I need you

You come when I call

You are so willing

To give me your all

Do I deserve it

Can I give to you

I know I don't have to

You don't demand it

But If I take it without return

I'm be no better than a bandit

Life - Love - Laughter
Del Pope

HAPPY BIRTHDAY KATHY
Twenty Seventh (Heaventh)

Happy Birthday Kathy
Many happy returns
May your troubles all diminish
As God's love light round you burns

Much love
Granddad Del

Life - Love - Laughter
Del Pope

PAIN IN YOUR HEART

How do you describe
The pain within your heart

When your most beloved
Says they soon will part

Life - Love - Laughter
Del Pope

TO BRUCE B.

Your children are not here

But some of your family are

This note is to ease the pain

Of a Fathers' Day afar.

Life - Love - Laughter
Del Pope

BORED

Am I bored
Yes I am
Sitting in my space

Tired of T V
Tired of radio
And a mirror with my face

Here I sit
In four walls
Trying to dispel

How I feel
How I look
When I'm not doing well

I must unglue
My bottom
From this old easy chair

And get myself
To heck outside
In sunlight and fresh air

Life - Love - Laughter
Del Pope

PEOPLE PASSING

The passing parade
Is fun to see
People passing
You and me

Where are they going
Why do they rush
Like a covey of quail
Into the brush

What are their thoughts
Are they happy or sad
Are they carrying good news
Or is it bad.

I hope it's happy
For life's too short
To be a constant
Worry wart.

Life should be fun
And full of love
Akin to that from up above

Look here comes one
With look perplexed
As if to say
What's coming next

But, not to worry
Not to fret
For the best is likely
Coming yet.

Life - Love - Laughter
Del Pope

The Lord is good
And he is just
You will prevail
If Him you trust.

So march along
In your parade
And don't you ever
Be afraid.

Life - Love - Laughter
Del Pope

WEDDING IN THE PARK
To David and Jo Beth Swingles

The couple said their marriage vows
Beneath the weeping willows boughs
Beside the lake the air was fresh
As the beauties of nature began to mesh
The sunlight shining was so soft
The birds sweetly singing all aloft
The music played so very mellow
Fell on ears hungrily fallow
It was a wedding in the park
Cupid's arrow found its mark
The sweet young couple were so eager
To say I do so he could kiss her
Their love light shone for all to see
And it affected all, even me
Many eyes were getting misty
No exception mine, kind of weepy
Any wedding is rather touching
With many hands a hanky clutching
But oh, this wedding in the park
Where love abounded in each heart
As many remembered weddings past
Praying this marriage long would last
So now God bless this bride and groom
May their love grow, prosper and bloom

Life - Love - Laughter
Del Pope

THE RECORDERS

I sat in awe as I first heard
The tones which sounded like a bird
The wooden instruments so like flutes
Made my ears open and my lips mute

They're called recorders I am told
And they date back to days of old
When they were used to train a bird
To sing the music that he heard

With tones so mellow and so sweet
I vibrate and thrill from head to feet
And I am sure that this great pleasure
Will stay a part of my minds treasure

Life - Love - Laughter
Del Pope

GRACIES HEART

They said the time had come
When we must do our thing
And open up your heart
To make your valves real clean

Well they can operate
And open up your chest
But I've got news for them
Your friends know this the best

Gracie's heart is all heart
But it's not in her chest
Her heart is her whole being
Her friends say not in jest

For Gracie's always giving
Her heart and all her best
To help some other person
To give their life some zest

Oh Gracie is not perfect
But her heart sure is
And no amount of surgery
Can find out where it is

It's way down deep
In her very soul
Waiting to help some one
Climb out of some dark hole

Life - Love - Laughter
Del Pope

Well here's to Gracie
I wish for her the best
So join with me and say a prayer
To give our Gracie rest

To make her well and bring her back
To all her loving friends
Who'll find no better heart than Gracie's
From here to this world's ends

Life - Love - Laughter
Del Pope

GRACIES GRATITUDE

This is from Gracie
To all of you
Who've stood by me
While things looked blue

Your love has helped
More than you know
To make me feel better
And my heart to glow

So now I say
With great concern
Though I know much
I've much to learn

Of friends and kindness
And their great love
It's so much like
The Father's above

                Thank you all
                    Gracie

Life - Love - Laughter
Del Pope

M K

You are quite a lady
I must admit
You're tender and kind
But have lots of grit

I admire your style
Your poise and grace
They go so well
With your lovely face

Life - Love - Laughter
Del Pope

HAPPY MOMENTS

Picking wild berries wet with morning dew
Flying a kite on a hill
Your first kiss
Happy birthday
The end of school
Being caressed by your mother
Being praised by your father
Your first sexual experience
Your sixteenth birthday
Your twenty first birthday
Getting married
Your first child
Income tax refund
Christmas
Riding a bike
Learning to drive
Your first car
Seeing a falling star
Forgiving someone
Kissing and making up
Swimming nude
Walking hand in hand
Sunrise Sunset
Locating the North Star
Seeing a rainbow
Homemade ice cream
Thanksgiving
The Fourth of July and fireworks
Water skiing
Sailing
Making love
Playing make believe

Life - Love - Laughter
Del Pope

Sniffing roses
Feeling silk or satin
Your first suit or formal dressGraduation
Beautiful music
Beautiful people
Going barefoot
Ad infinitum

Life - Love - Laughter
Del Pope

CRYSTAL PENDANT

A lead crystal pendant
For your patio door
Hang it in the sun
And watch its' many colors
Red, blue, green yellow
And many many more
They flash and dart,
Twirl and arc
Your twinkling eye follows
A fantasy of rainbow hues
To delight and amuse you
My pleasure at your thrill
Is worth my getting used to

Life - Love - Laughter
Del Pope

ODE TO ALICE

Who is Alice? We all know

She's the one who loves us so.

Her heart is warm She sings so sweet

A nicer person you'll not meet

She's always friendly, outgoing too

HAPPY BIRTHDAY ALICE

From us to you

Life - Love - Laughter
Del Pope

WHEN I AM NINETY

When I am ninety
I hope that I
Can be as spry
As Alice Netzen
Seems to be
For if I were
You would see
A guy who's acting
Not his age
As though he were
Upon a stage

Life - Love - Laughter
Del Pope

TELEPHONE

Why don't you ring when I need you
Instead of while I'm showering,
Or cooking my favorite dinner
When my appetite is towering

You ring when I'm making love.
You ring when I'm asleep.
But, when I'm lonesome and really need you
A silent vigil you keep.

Why don't you ring when I'm happy,
To make me happier still,
Instead of for bill collectors
Whose manners make me ill

Or, for friends who ask for favors
And never give one back.
Their lack of consideration
Is exceeded by lack of tact

Maybe I'm just touchy,
Or a little bit up tight,
But wouldn't you be if your phone only rang
In the middle of the night

Wrong number Who is this
Why me Lord It's too much.
All I wanted was conversation
And a gentle vocal touch.

Well, I must control my emotions
And be patient a little longer.
Someone nice will call me
And be a pleasant telephoner.

Life - Love - Laughter
Del Pope

WHAT IS LIFE

What is life here on earth
A span of time from death to birth
For preparation and experience
For acquaintance and endurance

To know a human in great depth
To know the world from length to breadth
And to feel with great emotion
A special love for mount and ocean

To run the gaunt of intense feeling
While your weakness you're revealing
And your strength to build and flex
So that life will not perplex

Do some deeds that are so good
Develop your character as you should
Nay I deny my first remark
Life is not all grim and dark

But interspersed with sunlight bright
And love to brighten up your night
To hold so close one who is dear
Whose heart your heart can feel so near

How great is real companionship
And someone's trust within your grip
All these things help to reveal
What is life and what is real

Should we be happy, should we be sad
Should we be good, should we be bad
Should we be great, should we be small
Should we love self, should we love all
All these things ring so true
To help to find the soul of you

Life - Love - Laughter
Del Pope

PENGUIN CAFE

Penguins are creatures
Who walk with a waddle

It kind of looks like
They've been hitting the bottle

They are permanently dressed
In a fresh clean tuxedo

Their home is a long way
From the city of Toledo

There is a café
In Laguna Beach

That uses their name
It's within easy reach

On south Coast Highway
Nine Eighty One

Your tummy is full
When their work is done

Life - Love - Laughter
Del Pope

WRITERS CHRISTMAS PARTY

They said write a poem
Well here it is.
It's about Christmas
And your best wish.

About relatives and friends
Who brighten you life.
About a good husband
Or a dutiful wife

It's about God's goodness
And Jesus' birth
To bring good cheer
In heaven and on earth

Life - Love - Laughter
Del Pope

DREAM GIRL

The girl in my dream
Was beautiful and sweet
She was happy and carefree
Even had pretty feet

'Twas a thrill being with her
A fantasy come true
All the feelings I was feeling
Seemed so real and brand new

She melted in my arms
And snuggled up close
My head was really spinning
Like heaven 'Twas the most

I could hear bells ringing
I had heard that one might
Nuts It's only the telephone
Shooting me down in mid flight

Life - Love - Laughter
Del Pope

FATAL FLAW

One daughter now
Is old enough you see
To start returning
Some advice to me

She has grown children
And has learned a lot
Just like I did
When I was a young 'Pop'

Suddenly I'm single
After many many years
And I am faced with
Unreasoning fears

All alone and
Searching for myself
With desperation
Hoping for some help

And there she is
All grown and mature
Saying Dad I'll help
She's such a dear

I'm getting acquainted
With many a lady

Who also have problems
Some very weighty

Some are pretty
And some are not
Some are bitchy

Life - Love - Laughter
Del Pope

And some are hot.

Some almost perfect
But with one flaw
So great it ruins
The good you saw

A fatal flaw
My daughter feels
Is when all is right
But naught prevails

If they are selfish
Or insecure
Or introverted
Or immature

Or some other things
Like telling lies
That sort of hit you
Between the eyes

It's tantalizing
To be so close

And see such beauty
Become morose

Is it myself
Who is at fault
Am I old ugly
Or unappealing

Is it self pity
I am feeling
How shall I act

Life - Love - Laughter
Del Pope

What shall I do

To make a new me
For the world and you

She said to me
Relax   Be yourself
You wont be long
Upon the shelf

Someone is looking
Just like you
To start a life
All fresh and new

It only takes two
The world has many
Lonesome people who
Would give a plenty

To find a mate
With no fatal flaw
Who sees in you
What in her you saw

And make your heart
Step up its' beat
And hope that you
Are ready to reap

The reward that comes
From persistence
And someone else's
Kind assistance

Life - Love - Laughter
Del Pope

And as you hold
The one that's new
Close to the heart
Pounding in you

Do you dare
Can you trust
Is it love
Is it lust

Will she remain
What you saw
Or will there be
A Fatal Flaw

Life - Love - Laughter
Del Pope

NOT TO LOVE

Not to love

Is not to live

Life - Love - Laughter
Del Pope

WHAT SOME MEN EXPECT OF A WIFE

TO LOOK LIKE A GIRL

ACT LIKE A LADY

THINK LIKE A MAN

WORK LIKE A DOG

Author unknown

Life - Love - Laughter
Del Pope

LONESOME GONE

I'm so lonesome
Oh my God
I miss you so
As alone I trod
We were so close
And needed each other
Now it's all gone
No need to bother
No shallow pretense
Of happy feelings
It's all so hollow
My head is reeling
I must resist
The quicksand of guilt
It just fell apart
The life that we built
Now you have a new love
And say you are happy
While I'm still looking
For someone who's snappy
Who'll look at me
With a twinkle in her eye
And say to me
You're my kind of guy
Then with no warning
One bright sunny day
There she is looking radiant
My sky's no longer gray
Her eyes so blue
Her hair so gold
She looks at me
Seems kind of bold
Not a word was said
We fell in love
With the nod of a head

Life - Love - Laughter
Del Pope

What a difference
Love can make
My world became steady
And ceased to shake
No more lonesome
No more blue
No more just me
Now me and you

Life - Love - Laughter
Del Pope

BROKE

Is this what it's like
To be broke
Your stomach thinks someone
Cut your throat
Your pockets are empty
Your spirit is down
You feel you don't know
A soul in town
Where are your friends
Who shared your money
They are so scarce
It's not even funny

Life - Love - Laughter
Del Pope

NICOLE

I'm a poet so I should know
You're poetry in motion
Wherever you go.
So sure and competent
And soft as a breeze
Your smile and manner
Puts me at ease.
Your eyes are warm
Your spirit bright
May your dreams be pleasant
Thru each long night.

Life - Love - Laughter
Del Pope

TAMMY

I didn't know her very well
Though we had met before
I guess it takes a little while
To really know the score
She's kinda small and petite
A very busy mother
Her disposition is so sweet
My comfort is no bother
Her heart is bigger than her body
She'd rather give than receive
Well, most of the time that is
Her friends seem to believe
Her hospitality comes so easy
You're made to feel at ease
To be received into her heart
Really is a breeze
So let me thank her with this poem
Though trite it somehow seems
I think I shall remember her
In very pleasant dreams.

Life - Love - Laughter
Del Pope

I'D RATHER BE AN EAGLE

I'd rather be a sparrow than a vulture

But if I had my choice

I'd rather be an eagle

And then I'd raise my voice

As in the sky I'd soar

And communicate with God

As I fly near heavens door.

Life - Love - Laughter
Del Pope

LOVE LOST

I must survive

I MUST SURVIVE!

But it hurts so much

Life - Love - Laughter
Del Pope

FULFILLING LOVE

To love is so fulfilling
Even if it's not returned

It's better to give than receive
That's a lesson I have learned

Giving love is like giving honey
If you try it you will find

You always get some on yourself
Somehow it's returned in kind

USE IT OR LOSE IT

As you grow older, you will find

You must stay active, body and mind

If you don't stay active and limber

You'll soon be stiff as an old timber

Your mind will soon grow so sluggish

You'll think it has turned into rubbish.

Life - Love - Laughter
Del Pope

OLD ACQUAINTANCE

Should old acquaintance be forgot
Emphatically I say no
Friends are made through pain and time
I hate to see one go
What is a friend I ask myself
While searching deep inside
It's someone who when chips are down
Says I'm still on your side
We need good friends and they need us
Believe me when I say
If you're a friend, when you need them
The sun shines on your day
Just remember as you use them
How good it really is
Because you never really know
When the next turn will be his.

Life - Love - Laughter
Del Pope

TOMATO WORM

The tomato worm is sneaky
He comes when you're not there
And eats the leaves and makes a mess
The plant is in despair

You look for him with no success
His green color makes it easy to hide
He molds himself to the twig
Until yourself you are beside

The only good thing I can say
Is his taste is kind of picky
He only eats the green leaves
And for this I feel so lucky

I love to eat the tomatoes
So let him eat the leaves
I'll eat the tomatoes then destroy the plant
And then we'll see who grieves

THIS TENDER FEELING

What is this tender feeling
That sets my senses reeling
And puts my defenses in disarray
Is it a new love stealing
My mind and inner being
With heart and soul held at bay
Knowing not the meaning
Of the thoughts you are beaming
But it seems to make my day

Life - Love - Laughter
Del Pope

COME, WRITE A POEM

Come, write a poem
Say what you are thinking.
Your writing has suffered
By your inspirational sinking.
You say it must be inspired
To make you able to write it,
Or maybe your poetic lethargy
Convinced you, you couldn't fight it.
Well look, you are writing
And maybe to no import
But to literate inactivity
You are making a retort.
Perhaps it will help to try to write daily
Could be talent will come home
Quicker than Bill Bailey.

Life - Love - Laughter
Del Pope

PERFECTION

Perfection is a word
Which folks throw around
When it suits their fancy
To put someone down

Perfection is what
They want you to be
While they get off
Totally Scott free

For to them perfection
Is too much trouble
They'd rather use it
To burst your bubble

Then they feel easy
At your expense
While they just sit
A-stride the fence

Of do nothing
And expect a lot
Well be a patsy for them
I will not.

Life - Love - Laughter
Del Pope

THE POWER OF GOD

The power of god
Has awed great men
Where man's power stops
His power begins

His reach is wide
His depth is chasmal
His sheltering hand
Still covers all

His love is true
His love is endless
His love covers sin
His love is in us

Don't bury this love
But let it shine
It will brighten your life
Which will brighten mine.

Life - Love - Laughter
Del Pope

SECRET AGE

So I forgot your birthday
What a shame
Well look at it this way
In a different frame
Your age is unknown
A mystery to me
To forget the age
I forget both
You see.

Life - Love - Laughter
Del Pope

TO JULIE - HAPPY 23RD

Birthdays are great
When you are young,
But wait till most
Of your song is sung.
You'll start to skip one
Now and then
And hope your figure
Stays nice and thin.
So enjoy them now
While you still can
And find yourself
The right kinda man,
Who '11 love you even
If you're fat
And still say, "Honey
I like all that."
And give yourself
To him in earnest
While you still have
Fire in your furnace.
Too soon you're old
And kinda flustered
And wondering, "Can I
Still cut the mustard."
Well shout it out
And say real clear
I'll cut it today
And again next year.

Life - Love - Laughter
Del Pope

ODE TO TERRE

Terre dear this is for you
Meaningful friendships are very few.
But I am one and you to me
A beautiful friendship I can see.
I care for you in a special way
You are closer to me every day
This friendship that I feel
Is vibrant and vital and very real
Lean on me with your cares
You won't catch me unawares
Because I think of you so much
I long to feel your gentle touch
Please don't be scared or insecure
All my motives are very pure
I know you're deep and so complex
Some others angers you would vex
But I have patience with your complexity
And long to help in your perplexity
Sometimes I feel so inadequate
To reach and fight off your advocate
But please believe me when I say
My prayers are with you every day
For God to love and hold you near
And heal your hurts and calm your fear
How good it was when I needed aid
To be held by a friend and not be afraid
So let this season and the next to come
Find you well and feeling calm.

Life - Love - Laughter
Del Pope

TAX TIME

The way you care

And the way you

Show it is very

Pleasing to me.

Thank you for Praying

And thank you

For staying 'til

IRS sets me

Free.

Life - Love - Laughter
Del Pope

TO CAROL

Some days are happy
Some days are bad.
And good times
Come and go.

But, keep on smiling
Whatever betides
And carry on
With the show.

Your friends still
Love you
And wish you well
This we want you to know.

And may these Flowers
And our good
Wishes
Bring to your heart
A warm glow.

Life - Love - Laughter
Del Pope

ODE TO GWENN

This ode's to Gwenn
A girl I know
Who comes from Canada
Up near the snow

Her charm is special
And kind a neat
Her presence cheers me
And feels so sweet

She came my way
Without my effort
And makes each day
A pleasure of sort

I hope that I
Can in some way
Make her day better
Along the way

For she is worthy
Of my time
And it's my pleasure
To make this rhyme.

Life - Love - Laughter
Del Pope

SHY

I don't look shy but I am
Though my face says I Am bold.

I sit back and shrink
And quake,

While I think of
Ways not to seem cold.

My heart is warm and outgoing
While a smile here and there I am throwing.
But when it's retumed
By a stranger I'm tumed,

To an ember that barely
Is glowing.

Life - Love - Laughter
Del Pope

DESPERATION

In desperation
  I counted on my fingers
Whom to call -
  To turn to -
Reach out for -
  To cling to
Seven
      Eight
            Nine
  People to hold close
Nine
    seven
        four
           none
Mistaken
    I had been in desperation
    finding others wouldn't do.
I ONLY WANTED HIM.

Author unknown
(Found in apartment trash bin)

Life - Love - Laughter
Del Pope

MY SPECIAL DAD

I sure love my special Dad
He makes me happy when I am sad
Oh what a friend he can be
When there's no one else I'd rather see

We get together every Thursday
To reminisce or go out to play
Dad's like mine are hard to come by
I'll never trade mine and that's no lie

Thank you Dad for your understanding
You've made my life an easy landing
To be your daughter makes me glad
Forever you'll be my special Dad

by Dee Ann Pope

Life - Love - Laughter
Del Pope

MY MOTHER – MY FRIEND

January 5th is a very special day,
For on this day was born my Mother.
A very special person in every way ,
Above her there could be no other.

Out of Love she gave birth to me,
Giving to me Love, Joy, Challenge & Wonder.
How lucky I am her daughter to be,
Having unconditional Love & Friendship from her.

I love her deeply more than words can say,
And treasure every moment together we spend.
With love I wish a special Happy Birthday,
To a very special woman, My Mother –
My Friend.

by Dee Ann Pope
01/05/1998

Life - Love - Laughter
Del Pope

A NEW HEART

You loved a heart

That had stopped beating

Built a shelter

To keep it warm

Took time to put the pieces together

My heart belongs to you

Our hearts will beat together

Forever with our love

by Lil Semanski

Life - Love - Laughter
Del Pope

INDEX

Book Page
1. HAPPINESS IS AN ATTITUDE
2. ONE DAY AT A TIME
3. TO LOVE A FRIEND
4. LIVE EACH DAY
5. INTROSPECT
7. TO LISA A CHLORASEPTIC JUNKIE
8. IRS/GESTAPO
9. DEAR MOM AND DAD
10. BIG BEAR LAKE
11. LOVE REQUITED
12. DORIS
13. CHRISTMAS CHEER
14. THE GOOD YEARS
16. A DAUGHTER NAMED DEE
17. FLU
18. I'M A LEAF
19. ODE TO MARY NEWLANDS
20. POETRY
21. RAINBOW
22. SEARCH FOR TRUE LOVE
23. THE SEA AND ME
25. ODE TO HELEN
26. MY DEAR OLD DAD
28. LOW EBB
29. JANE JANE
30. HELLO
31. BECKY THE COBBLER AND THE ELF
32. DARE TO DREAM
33. WILL I LOVE AGAIN
34. THE WAY SHE LOOKS TO ME
35. SAN DIEGO AT NIGHT
37. TRIBUTE TO MARY NEWLANDS
39. HAPPY MOTHERS DAY M K
40. EXCEPTIONAL PERSON
41. A MISTAKE OF LOVE

Life - Love - Laughter
Del Pope

43.	CHRISTMAS IN CALIFORNIA
44.	PEACEFUL EVENING
45.	JUDY G.
46.	BIRTHDAYS
47.	HERPES SYMPLEX PARANOIA
48.	LOVE YOU
49.	I BELIEVE
51.	BEVERLY HARNDEN
52.	HAPPY BIRTHDAY MARY D.
53.	LIGHT OF MY LIFE
54.	HAPPY BIRTHDAY, KATHY
55.	PAIN IN YOUR HEART
56.	TO BRUCE B
57.	BORED
58.	PEOPLE PASSING
60.	WEDDING IN THE PARK
61.	THE RECORDERS
62.	GRACIE'S HEART
64.	GRACIE'S GRATITUDE
65.	M K
66.	HAPPY MOMENTS
68.	CRYSTAL PENDANT
69.	ODE TO ALICE
70.	WHEN I AM NINETY
71.	TELEPHONE
72.	WHAT IS LIFE
73.	PENGUIN CAFÉ
74.	WRITERS CHRISTMAS PARTY
75.	DREAM GIRL
76.	FATAL FLAW
80.	NOT TO LOVE
81.	WHAT SOME MEN EXPECT OF A WIFE
82.	LONESOME GONE
84.	BROKE
85.	NICOLE
86.	TAMMY
87.	I'D RATHER BE AN EAGLE

88.	LOVE LOST
88.	FULFILLING LOVE
90.	USE IT OR LOSE IT
91	OLD ACQUAINTANCE
92	TOMATO WORM
93	HIS TENDER FEELING
94	COME, WRITE A POEM
95	PERFECTION
96	THE POWER OF GOD
97	SECRET AGE
98	TO JULIE HAPPY 23RD
99	ODE TO TERRE
100.	TAX TIME
101.	TO CAROL
102.	ODE TO GWENN
103.	SHY
104.	DESPERATION
105.	MY SPECIAL DAD
106.	MY MOTHER MY FRIEND
107.	A NEW HEART

Life - Love - Laughter
Del Pope

ABOUT THE AUTHOR

Del Pope was born near Warner, Muskogee County, Oklahoma into a family of cowboy boot makers and leather workers. At eight years old, they moved to Borger, Texas, a rowdy oil boom town, where he got his schooling into High School. By fifteen, his father said, "This is your business college," and sent him to run a shoe shop in Sunray, Texas about fifty miles from home.

Del married at nineteen and has since lived in 7 states and now settled in Mission Viejo California. He studied music and Christian Ministry at Pacific Bible College at Portland Oregon and Business Administration at the University of Hawaii.

At this writing, he's eighty five years old and works as a handy man five to six days a week.

Del is a member of Los Escribientes Writers Club and currently writing his autobiography.

www.ingramcontent.com/pod-product-compliance
Lightning Source LLC
Chambersburg PA
CBHW071259040426
42444CB00009B/1792